New Proficiency Reading: an overview

New Proficiency Reading offers systematic training in the reading skills required for the Reading Paper of the Revised Cambridge Proficiency examination. Students are guided through strategies that will help them to read texts effectively and answer the exam questions correctly. It includes a wide variety of authentic texts including books (fiction and nonfiction), magazines, newspapers, non-specialist articles from journals, publicity and informational materials (e.g. advertisements, guide books, manuals). These texts accurately reflect the level of the Revised Proficiency examination and cover the major topic areas. *New Proficiency Reading* also provides comprehensive vocabulary development organised in themes commonly tested in the exam.

The tasks in *New Proficiency Reading* will help students to:

- become familiar with a wide range of sources, registers, topics and lexical fields.
- become sensitive to meaning in words and lexical combinations, including idioms and phrasal verbs.
- understand the overall function and message of texts.
- analyse the global organisation of a text.
- explore the way parts of a text are related, e.g. premise/conclusion.
- understand the gist of a text, even if some words are unknown.
- isolate specific information in a text.
- recognise and evaluate attitude and opinion.
- infer underlying meaning in a text.

Organisation of the book

New Proficiency Reading is divided into four cycles. Each cycle contains four units and provides guidance and practice in all four parts of the Revised Cambridge Proficiency Reading Paper.

Each unit focuses on one of the parts in the Reading Paper. The unit always begins with an **Exam strategy** section in which students learn how to deal with irony and figurative language, how to cope with unfamiliar words, how to infer meaning from the text, etc. By reading through the **skills check** boxes and working through the tasks in this section, students will become proficient at using the key reading skills needed to tackle the tasks in the examination successfully.

The **Exam strategy** section is followed by an **Exam practice** section. This contains exam level texts for one of the four parts of the Reading Paper so that students can further consolidate the particular skill they have learnt. **Exam tip** boxes provide useful hints on the best ways to tackle the **Exam practice** task.

Each unit ends with an extensive **Vocabulary development** section. This section develops students' range of vocabulary, particularly in such areas as collocation, idioms and expressions, word sets and phrasal verbs.

Unit map

The table below summarises the objectives of each unit section and makes suggestions about the teaching approach and lesson planning.

Unit section	Objectives	Assignment
Exam practice: skills check and text(s)	• To highlight a reading skill and to provide thorough training in it. • To develop an exam strategy by means of a **tip** box. • To provide thorough practice for the relevant part of the exam.	Done in class.
Exam practice: text(s)	• To provide further practice in a particular reading skill. • To provide practice in the relevant section of the exam.	Text(s) and questions prepared for homework and checked in class.
Vocabulary development	• To focus on vocabulary from the text(s) of the unit. • To provide contextualised practice on a range of lexical items including collocations, idioms and expressions, etc.	Done in class or can be set for homework.

Developing reading skills

The skills highlighted in the book are listed below:
- reading for gist
- dealing with unfamiliar words
- recognising text links
- identifying style and tone
- reading between the lines
- reading for detail
- answering multiple choice questions
- distinguishing the literal from the figurative
- increasing reading speed
- identifying irony

Progress Test 1 (Units 1–4)

Choose the best answer, A, B, C or D.

1 My brother is a real ..... potato. He watches TV all the time!
A couch   B sofa
C armchair   D cushion

2 It would be nice if I passed my exams but I don't hold ..... much hope.
A with   B up
C out   D onto

3 After three days in the desert, his mind began to play ..... on him.
A games   B jokes
C tricks   D fun

4 Come on. Spill the ..... ! What's the big secret?
A peas   B beans
C milk   D dust

5 Tina and her new classmate are getting on like a ..... on fire.
A tree   B pan
C bush   D house

6 We won't know the ..... extent of the damage for a few days.
A full   B whole
C utter   D absolute

7 Calm down! There's no need to ..... off the handle.
A fly   B jump
C run   D leap

8 The claims the woman made had a ..... of truth about them.
A ring   B mark
C shade   D circle

9 You haven't signed a contract yet, so it's not too late to back ..... the deal.
A into   B down from
C away from   D out of

10 Stop beating about the ..... and say what you really mean!
A table   B boat
C bush   D plot

11 Please don't ..... fun at me all the time!
A push   B poke
C pitch   D prod

12 I'm trying to arrange an interview with the editor but it's difficult to ..... him down to an exact time.
A stick   B fix
C pin   D glue

13 Don't mention politics to John; it's like a red ..... to a bull.
A cloth   B mat
C rag   D scarf

14 The girl ..... her friend with her elbow to draw her attention to what was happening.
A poked   B pointed
C nudged   D stroked

15 Finding the gorillas alive had been ..... his wildest dreams.
A past   B beneath
C beyond   D without

16 Coming top in the exam was a real ..... in her cap.
A feather   B plume
C badge   D medal

17 The leopard ..... its prey for hours before it finally went in for the kill.
A crouched   B crept
C scrambled   D stalked

18 In spite of his owner's cruelty, the dog ..... no grudge against humans.
A takes   B bears
C carries   D supports

19 The rabbits were kept outside the house in a large wooden ..... .
A hut   B warren
C hutch   D eyrie

20 Dave keeps going on about the evils of modern farming; he's got a real ..... in his bonnet about it.
A ant   B bee
C spider   D wasp

21 Brenda has an amazing appetite. She eats like a ..... .
A horse   B wolf
C whale   D lion

22 The keeper grabbed the lion cub by the ..... of its neck.
A mane   B fur
C scruff   D hide

23 Don't trust him. He's a real snake in the ..... .

  A nest   **B** grass

  C bush   **D** hole

24 By any ..... , a zoo keeper's job is a difficult one.

  A reasons   **B** levels

  C standards   **D** limits

25 Unless we act now, gorillas will become extinct, without a ..... of doubt.

  A hint   **B** tinge

  C ghost   **D** shadow

26 As the weather was bad, the tourists whiled ..... the time strolling round the local shops.

  A in   **B** off

  C up   **D** away

27 It took us some time to get to ..... with the crisis.

  A tongs   **B** claws

  C grips   **D** tacks

28 Fiona's enthusiasm for natural history ..... no bounds.

  A recognises   **B** holds

  C sees   **D** knows

29 The travel company went to ..... lengths to make their clients feel at home.

  A major   **B** great

  C far   **D** strong

30 Young people have a ..... to go rather wild while on holiday.

  A tendency   **B** habit

  C problem   **D** characteristic

31 We were completely ..... when we saw the terrible state of our hotel.

  A taken away   **B** taken aback

  C taken in   **D** taken away

32 By an unfortunate ..... , the tour company had omitted John's name from their list.

  A neglect   **B** disregard

  C insult   **D** oversight

33 The Embassy ..... against travelling in the remoter parts of the country.

  A emphasises   **B** advises

  C declares   **D** maintains

34 The hotel was flooded, so the tourists were housed in ..... accommodation.

  A makeshift   **B** conditional

  C brief   **D** tentative

35 The rooms had just been cleaned and looked ..... and span.

  A spit   **B** spin

  C spick   **D** speck

36 We're so busy at work that I have ..... booking a holiday for the time being.

  A refrained   **B** put off

  C held over   **D** waited

37 We ..... the coastline and then headed inland.

  A skirted   **B** sided

  C outlined   **D** edged

38 Don't let the tour operators take you ..... with their sales patter. None of it is true!

  A down   **B** in

  C along   **D** about

39 Because of bad weather, Samantha's flight was ..... .

  A undue   **B** unpunctual

  C overdue   **D** belated

40 Opportunities to travel are few and far ..... in my profession.

  A between   **B** off

  C beyond   **D** away

41 We need to come ..... the problem from a different angle.

  A to   **B** on

  C at   **D** by

42 Tom revealed his ..... for writing at a very early age.

  A faculty   **B** craft

  C expertise   **D** gift

43 I'm pleased to say that the baby is ..... with health!

  A bouncing   **B** skipping

  C hopping   **D** prancing

44 It's a long time since you saw her but this photo may ..... your memory.

  A jog   **B** juggle

  C jostle   **D** jam

45 The old lady dislocated her ..... , so she was confined to a wheelchair.

  A hip   **B** thigh

  C knuckle   **D** calf

Progress Test 2 (Units 5–8)

Choose the best answer, A, B, C or D.

1 Are you ..... for your driving test soon?
A going on   B going out
C going in   D going after

2 The stunt man ..... off his injury and finished the scene.
A shrugged   B threw
C carried   D put

3 The painter said that early failure had only ..... him on to greater efforts.
A inspired   B encouraged
C spurred   D approved

4 The actress is ..... starring in a new musical.
A lately   B recently
C presently   D currently

5 I recognise that singer's face but his name ..... me.
A fails   B evades
C deludes   D escapes

6 After the first half hour of the play, time began to ..... .
A delay   B drag
C extend   D relax

7 I wish the actors would speak up. I can't make ..... what they're saying.
A up   B out
C off   D over

8 Some romantic novelists ..... out books with the same old formula every year.
A churn   B spill
C ladle   D pour

9 Take it easy! There's no need to make such a ..... and dance about it.
A tune   B song
C verse   D drum

10 The book was really funny – it had me ..... stitches.
A in   B on
C at   D into

11 Don't believe him! He's just ..... your leg.
A shaking   B pulling
C poking   D kicking

12 We were ..... stiff as we walked through the deserted streets at midnight.
A scared   B frightened
C feared   D terrified

13 An apology would go a long ..... towards healing his wounded pride.
A time   B way
C distance   D road

14 I ran ..... one of your friends at the disco last night.
A over   B off
C by   D into

15 I wish you'd stop being such a wet ..... and join in the fun!
A blanket   B sheet
C towel   D pillow

16 It's no ..... my trying to learn Latin; it's just too difficult for me.
A worth   B point
C good   D reason

17 At a ..... guess, I'd say that Shakespeare wrote about 35 plays.
A brief   B rough
C ready   D round

18 No matter how angry you are, you should never ..... to violence.
A exert   B resort
C recourse   D resolve

19 You shouldn't ..... into other people's private lives.
A prowl   B prod
C proceed   D pry

20 I'm not surprised you can't find your notes. Your desk is ..... with papers!
A muddled   B bundled
C cluttered   D burdened

21 The windscreen of the school minibus was ..... in the accident.
A shattered   B tangled
C tattered   D dented

22 The head teacher has asked me to take the new boy under my ..... and look after him.
A wing   B arm
C cloak   D sleeves

23 You've signed the contract, so it's too late to back ..... now.
A on   B away
C out   D up

24 He will be sued for ..... of contract if he does not do what he promised.
A fracture   B crack
C rupture   D breach

25 That firm is a leader in the ..... of engineering.
A field   B area
C topic   D background

26 The documents vanished into ..... air.
A clean   B pure
C thin   D clear

27 In spite of working their fingers to the ..... , all the staff were made redundant.
A nail   B edge
C flesh   D bone

28 He was forced to sell the business ..... a loss.
A at   B for
C with   D on

29 Tom became very embittered when he was passed ..... for promotion.
A up   B off
C down   D over

30 Until business improves, the firm are only going to employ a ..... staff.
A skeleton   B bare
C reduced   D limited

31 It is ..... surprising that the company folded after all the problems they had.
A scarcely   B rarely
C aptly   D justly

32 Sandra's ..... sin is pride.
A redeeming   B overriding
C besetting   D overwhelming

33 Ben's success threatened to go to his ..... .
A mind   B senses
C head   D brains

34 Sheila was tempted to ..... in her notice straightaway.
A put   B write
C sign   D hand

35 The director tried to oppose the merger but it went ..... in the end.
A over   B ahead
C on   D up

36 The muggers got ..... away with my bag.
A completely   B long
C hard   D clean

37 Did he die of natural causes, or do the police suspect foul ..... ?
A game   B play
C act   D crime

38 I had some time to ..... , so I went and looked round the shops.
A attack   B hang
C strangle   D kill

39 That judge is feared because she takes a hard ..... in the fight against drugs.
A line   B lane
C path   D rule

40 The detective saw ..... the deception very quickly.
A through   B past
C into   D round

41 The man was ..... guilty of theft.
A condemned   B accused
C found   D convicted

42 There has been a(n) ..... of thefts in the town recently.
A rate   B influx
C tide   D spate

43 Tom is determined to ..... his name and prove his innocence.
A reprieve   B liberate
C wipe   D clear

44 My uncle has been ..... from driving for a year.
A forbidden   B banned
C excluded   D expelled

45 The suspect is being kept in police ..... while they question her further about the murder.
A custody   B guard
C control   D care

Progress Test 3 (Units 9–12)

Choose the best answer, A, B, C or D.

1 It was ….. dark in the cave.
A jet
B coal
C dark
D pitch

2 There is a ….. possibility that life will be found on Mars.
A plain
B distinct
C full
D sharp

3 The company was fined for failing to ….. with the law.
A comply
B obey
C abide
D acquiesce

4 His research ….. the way for further discoveries.
A granted
B planted
C paved
D laid

5 Testing drugs on animals is considered to be a necessary ….. by some scientists.
A sin
B evil
C shame
D wrong

6 I think I have done enough revision but the acid ….. will come when I sit the exam.
A proof
B test
C result
D answer

7 The portrait has been attributed ….. a Dutch master.
A about
B for
C to
D in

8 I'm not prepared to put ….. this noise any longer.
A up with
B up
C down to
D in for

9 You look as ….. as a fiddle!
A funny
B fit
C fat
D free

10 I wish my little sister weren't such a pain in the ….. !
A head
B heart
C foot
D neck

11 If you lay a ….. on my brother, I'll call the police.
A finger
B touch
C foot
D scratch

12 You should never look a gift ….. in the mouth.
A dog
B sheep
C horse
D cow

13 I thought something terrible had happened but it was all a ….. in a teacup.
A storm
B gale
C breeze
D wind

14 He put his life in ….. by driving so fast.
A stake
B hazard
C risk
D jeopardy

15 When it ….. to creative writing, he's a genius!
A turns
B reaches
C falls
D comes

16 Never in my ….. dreams did I imagine that this would happen!
A greatest
B maddest
C wildest
D best

17 They robbed the bank and made ….. with a great deal of money.
A away
B off
C out
D up

18 She was furious and looked ….. at him.
A daggers
B knives
C swords
D blades

19 Sharon was ….. to eat the cake but she managed to stop herself.
A induced
B tempted
C attracted
D persuaded

20 They ….. me off in that boutique! Things are much cheaper in the shop down the road.
A tore
B pulled
C ripped
D dragged

21 Sharing the housework is part and ….. of getting married.
A burden
B packet
C load
D parcel

22 Clare has always had a ….. on her shoulder about not going to university.
A cut
B mark
C stain
D chip

23 Peter is finding it very hard to ….. to married life.
A adjust
B reconcile
C concur
D accord

24 The thief gave the police the ….. and escaped.
A run
B slip
C turn
D edge

25 It was a cruel ….. of fate.
A twist
B screw
C turn
D leap

26 Petra gets very nervous on public occasions – she can hardly ….. two words together.
A line
B rope
C string
D pleat

27 Her nerves were torn to ..... .
A slits   B parts
C strips   D shreds

28 A cure for cancer may soon be within our ..... .
A clutch   B grip
C clasp   D grasp

29 Investigators are trying to ..... more light on the causes of the crash.
A shine   B shed
C reflect   D direct

30 We need to ..... out a few problems before launching the product on the market.
A flatten   B tidy
C iron   D clear

31 The idea of going into business ..... no appeal for me.
A makes   B holds
C provides   D consists

32 It is standard ..... for the company to refuse to give refunds without a receipt.
A routine   B custom
C practice   D process

33 After months of failure, the company finally ..... on a brilliant idea.
A hit   B burst
C struck   D shot

34 Although cautious in their approach, the production team is always ..... to new ideas.
A open   B enthusiastic
C welcome   D eager

35 If you want a good camera, there's nothing I ..... more highly than this model.
A recommend   B propose
C advise   D applaud

36 The results of the inquiry may lend ..... to the claims made by the scientist.
A gravity   B depth
C weight   D volume

37 The news that the company is to close ..... as no surprise to me.
A comes   B happens
C occurs   D appears

38 When people live in such close ..... to each other, there are bound to be occasional problems.
A neighbourhood B vicinity
C position   D proximity

39 Our rivals are making a takeover ..... for our firm.
A offer   B attempt
C bid   D deal

40 I'm afraid astronomy is a ..... book to me; I don't understand it at all.
A shut   B closed
C spent   D dull

41 We saw ..... details of the disaster on television last night.
A elaborate   B knotty
C graphic   D burning

42 The painting Sonya entered in the competition put mine in the ..... .
A shade   B dark
C shadow   D dusk

43 Our teacher is wonderful – she can put ..... the most difficult subject really clearly.
A out   B on
C forward   D over

44 My great-grandmother is as ..... as a post.
A blind   B daft
C deaf   D lame

45 When the stunt man heard what he had to do, he didn't turn a ..... !
A heel   B head
C finger   D hair

Progress Test 4 (Units 13–16)

Choose the best answer, A, B, C or D.

1 Tragedy ..... yesterday when a man was swept out to sea by a freak wave.
A struck   B sparked
C hit   D came

2 I'm feeling a bit ..... the weather today.
A over   B under
C below   D above

3 Are you having second ..... about going to the party?
A thoughts   B plans
C intentions   D ideas

4 Sam has turned over a new ..... ; he's a little angel these days!
A leaf   B life
C road   D page

5 I'm going to ..... in my mother's footsteps.
A follow   B march
C walk   D go

6 Let's have a drink to ..... the ice before we start the meeting.
A shatter   B split
C break   D fracture

7 I caught the train by the ..... of my teeth.
A edge   B run
C white   D skin

8 Cloning is a ..... debated issue.
A deeply   B hotly
C profoundly   D heavily

9 I guessed that answer but it was just a ..... in the dark.
A jump   B shot
C leap   D slap

10 Kate wears her heart on her ..... .
A jacket   B bracelet
C hat   D sleeve

11 Your fears about the future are often completely ..... .
A baseless   B pointless
C groundless   D aimless

12 Stick to your ..... and don't let anyone change your mind.
A bullets   B weapons
C guns   D pistols

13 I am not persuaded that our best interests ..... in developing new technologies like that.
A lie   B rest
C centre   D stand

14 My mother has to put ..... with all my bad habits.
A by   B up
C through   D round

15 It is important we do not ..... the wrong conclusions from these experiments.
A jump   B draw
C take   D gather

16 The ..... were stacked against them but they survived their ordeal.
A fates   B hopes
C odds   D chances

17 The lizard ..... in the warmth of the early morning sun.
A enjoyed   B relished
C basked   D absorbed

18 I eat sensibly and try to ..... clear of junk food.
A wind   B drive
C move   D steer

19 The ambulance arrived in the ..... of time.
A nick   B stroke
C point   D heat

20 The manager turned on her ..... and stormed out of the office.
A foot   B heel
C step   D spot

21 He won't take responsibility for the disaster. He will try to pass the ..... .
A fault   B burden
C buck   D problem

22 I'm a vegetarian. I refuse to eat meat on ..... .
A belief   B conscience
C principle   D theory

23 She's threatening to cause trouble but I think we should ..... her bluff.
A make   B do
C see   D call

24 The new shopping centre looks awful! In my opinion, it's a blot ..... the landscape.
A in   B on
C at   D for

25 I wish you wouldn't ..... up a fuss about such a minor mistake!
A take   B make
C kick   D beat

26 Although we agree on the main issues, we still differ on some ..... of detail.
A lists   B items
C points   D articles

27 Plans to build a new shopping centre have been ..... by the local authorities.

| **A** put down | **B** run down |
| **C** turned down | **D** talked down |

28 I thought I'd lost my wallet but it turned ..... in the end.

| **A** in | **B** over |
| **C** by | **D** up |

29 I hate people who sit on the ..... and never take a position on an issue.

| **A** sofa | **B** fence |
| **C** bench | **D** bank |

30 They've decided to ..... the hatchet and make up their quarrel.

| **A** pass | **B** carry |
| **C** bury | **D** drop |

31 It's too late to do anything now. You've ..... the boat, I'm afraid.

| **A** lost | **B** missed |
| **C** sunk | **D** forgotten |

32 When I said I could do the job, I probably bit off more than I could ..... .

| **A** swallow | **B** eat |
| **C** devour | **D** chew |

33 That's not real – it's just a ..... of your imagination.

| **A** bit | **B** figure |
| **C** picture | **D** figment |

34 Martha was very upset. I think she was on the ..... of tears when I left.

| **A** edge | **B** verge |
| **C** side | **D** margin |

35 Sarah thinks she can set the world to ..... all by herself.

| **A** justice | **B** fairness |
| **C** rights | **D** principles |

36 Who was the first person to ..... the Egyptian hieroglyphic script?

| **A** decode | **B** decipher |
| **C** deconstruct | **D** delineate |

37 The car crashed because someone had ..... with the brakes.

| **A** serviced | **B** altered |
| **C** tampered | **D** tricked |

38 Our plan failed, so it's back to the drawing ..... , I'm afraid!

| **A** room | **B** board |
| **C** table | **D** pin |

39 I don't know what our guests will want to do this weekend. We'll have to play it by ..... .

| **A** ear | **B** eye |
| **C** mouth | **D** hand |

40 I hope all your hard work ..... fruit.

| **A** brings | **B** has |
| **C** makes | **D** bears |

41 Fossils like this are only discovered once in a ..... moon.

| **A** red | **B** blue |
| **C** yellow | **D** pink |

42 We'll have to burn the midnight ..... if we want to finish this project on time.

| **A** oil | **B** coal |
| **C** fire | **D** spirit |

43 When I started to study archaeology, I knew ..... no Latin, but within a year I could read it rather well.

| **A** barely | **B** entirely |
| **C** scarcely | **D** virtually |

44 The historian has just brought ..... a book on the Second World War.

| **A** up | **B** on |
| **C** out | **D** over |

45 When I was a teenager, I had a ..... on one of my teachers.

| **A** fondness | **B** passion |
| **C** fancy | **D** crush |

Answer Key

Exam strategy: Part 1 (pp. 4-5)

A (p. 4)
Number 2 is the best summary.

B (p. 4)
Question 1 = a   Question 4 = c
Question 2 = b   Question 5 = a
Question 3 = e   Question 6 = d

C (p. 5)
1 B; 2 C; 3 A; 4 B; 5 D; 6 C

D (p. 5)
It is about the qualities that a good newspaper editor needs.

E (p. 5)
1 C; 2 A

F (p. 5)
3 A; 4 B; 5 C; 6 C

Exam practice: Part 1 (pp. 6–7)

Reporting the news (p. 6)
1 C; 2 B; 3 D; 4 A; 5 D; 6 B

Taste (p. 6)
7 D; 8 C; 9 B; 10 A; 11 C; 12 D

Lost in the tangled forest (p. 7)
13 B; 14 A; 15 D; 16 A; 17 D; 18 C

Vocabulary development (pp. 8–11)

A Descriptive adjectives (p. 8)
1 unbending; 2 satirical; 3 condescending;
4 menacing; 5 flippant; 6 antagonistic; 7 biased;
8 grudging; 9 sceptical; 10 overbearing

B Similar but different (p. 8)
1 emanate; 2 let; 3 dead; 4 sorely; 5 modest;
6 turn; 7 on the grounds; 8 keeping; 9 sharp;
10 assigning

C Phrasal verbs with *hold* (p. 9)
1 held down; 2 held up; 3 hold (you) to;
4 hold onto; 5 hold up; 6 hold out; 7 hold with;
8 is holding (it) against; 9 held up;
10 holding out for

D Common expressions (p. 9)
1 d; 2 a; 3 h; 4 c; 5 g; 6 b; 7 f; 8 e; 9 j; 10 i

1 burnt his boats
2 beat about the bush
3 bites/bit the dust
4 do a bunk
5 jump the gun
6 fly off the handle
7 is barking up the wrong tree
8 calling a spade a spade
9 Spill the beans
10 is jumping on the bandwagon

E Similes (p. 10)
1 like a hawk
2 like a Trojan
3 like a bad penny
4 like a house on fire
5 like a bull in a china shop
6 like a bear with a sore head
7 like a ton of bricks
8 like a sieve
9 like a trooper
10 like wildfire
11 like a red rag to a bull
12 like water off a duck's back
13 like a rhinoceros
14 like looking for a needle in a haystack
15 like a log
16 like a shot
17 like the back of his hand
18 like a drowned rat
19 like a Cheshire cat
20 like something the cat brought in

F Prepositions (p. 11)
1 for; 2 about; 3 of; 4 out; 5 of; 6 off; 7 at;
8 in; 9 with; 10 in

G Collocations (p. 11)
1 e; **2** f; **3** a; **4** g; **5** d; **6** c; **7** h; **8** b

1 wonder woman; **2** plastic surgeon; **3** tin god;
4 casualty department; **5** game show; **6** tabloid
newspaper; **7** obstacle course; **8** couch potato

UNIT 2 — Creatures great and small

Exam strategy: Part 2 (pp. 12–13)

A (p. 12)
Author of text:
Attenborough, Sir David (born 1926)
English naturalist and broadcaster, born in London.
Well-known for his documentary film-making,
including series which have been immensely popular
worldwide like 'Life on Earth' and 'The Living Planet'.

B (p. 12)
1 The vocabulary in Text 1 is fairly technical (as
shown by words like 'ossicles' and 'scutes'). In Text
2 it is not technical.
2 In Text 1 there is one very complex sentence (the
last sentence). In Text 2 the sentences are not
complex.
3 Text 1 was written to inform. Text 2 was written
both to inform and also to appeal to the reader's
emotions.
4 Text 1 is written for either the specialist or the
interested layman. Text 2 is written for the general
reader.
5 In Text 1 the author's style is neutral and factual. In
Text 2 it is more emotive.

C (p. 13)
Author of text:
Durrell, Gerald (1925–1995)
Author and naturalist. 'My Family and Other Animals'
and other novels describe his childhood in Corfu. He
founded the Jersey Wildlife Preservation Trust, which
has made an important contribution to the
preservation of endangered species. Brother of novelist
Laurence Durrell.

D (p. 13)
Students should underline the following:
… I realised I was rearing a monster.
*Potsil lived to eat and would fall upon anything, living
or dead, that came within reach.*
*There was nothing he would not throw himself onto
with screams of joy, … as being inedible.*
*His greatest ambition in life was to consume a human
being … beyond his abilities.*

The writer exaggerates to bring out the humour of the
situation.

E (p. 13)
1 B; **2** C

Exam practice: Part 2 (pp. 14–17)

Killer whales (p. 14)
1 A; **2** D

Dolphin talk (p. 15)
3 C; **4** B

Play – fun or primitive instinct? (p. 16)
5 C; **6** D

Animal intelligence (p. 17)
7 B; **8** C

Vocabulary development (pp. 18–21)

A Animal groups (p. 18)
1 d/f; **2** c; **3** e; **4** b; **5** f; **6** a

B Animal homes (p. 18)
1 d; **2** f; **3** a; **4** b; **5** g; **6** e; **7** h; **8** c

C Animal families (p. 18)
1 f; **2** d; **3** a; **4** b; **5** c; **6** e

D Parts of an animal's body (pp. 18–19)
a
1 b; **2** h; **3** f; **4** j; **5** g; **6** i; **7** a; **8** c; **9** d; **10** e

b
1 the scales dropped from her eyes
2 his jaw dropped
3 by the skin of her teeth
4 has got her claws into
5 The fur began to fly
6 a feather in his cap
7 I haven't seen hide nor hair of
8 ruffled Fiona's feathers

E Similar but different (p. 19)
1 untold; **2** carcass; **3** contribution; **4** lethal;
5 virulent; **6** reputed; **7** successor; **8** notoriously;
9 banned; **10** coaxed; **11** in retrospect;
12 face to face

F Prepositions (p. 19)
1 under; **2** without; **3** below; **4** beyond; **5** over;
6 beneath; **7** within; **8** in

G Ways of communicating (p. 20)

a

buzz: bee, bumblebee

croak: frog

drone: bee

growl: dog, lion, tiger, bear

purr: cat

roar: big cat (e.g. lion, tiger)

whine: dog

b

1 purred; **2** droned; **3** croaked; **4** whining; **5** roaring; **6** growled

H Phrasal verbs with *take* (p. 20)

1 be taken in; **2** took (it) in; **3** take out (your bad mood) on; **4** took (it) on/upon; **5** take to; **6** has taken up/took up; **7** was taken aback; **8** take off; **9** takes after; **10** took down

I Verb and noun collocations (p. 20)

assume a posture	nod one's head
bear a resemblance	rear offspring
exchange a glance	sound the alarm
inflict a wound	stifle a yawn
jog somebody's memory	take a hint
make a stab (at)	utter a sound

J Verbs of movement (p. 21)

1 stalked; **2** leapt/leaped; **3** crept; **4** scrambled; **5** pounced; **6** lurking; **7** crouched

K Similar but different (p. 21)

1 drawing; **2** casts; **3** lightning; **4** mixed; **5** scruff; **6** aback; **7** prey; **8** goose; **9** newly; **10** fittest

---

UNIT

3 Going places

Exam strategy: Part 3 (pp. 22–23)

A (p. 22)

Author of text:

Theroux, Paul Edward (born 1941)

American novelist and travel writer. He has travelled widely through Asia and America. He is an intelligent, witty observer of life in these countries.

B (p. 22)

1 oil; **2** smoke; **3** slopes; **4** wood; **5** clean; **6** sound/noise; **7** fall/break; **8** prehistoric; **9** wind; **10** flood

C (p. 23)

1 C; **2** A; **3** D

D (p. 23)

B was not needed. The only person in the main text to which 'He' in the first sentence could refer is the one before gap 3. However, Paragraph B cannot fit here because the paragraph immediately after begins: 'Yet this old train …'. Therefore the missing paragraph must make reference to a train rather than to a person.

Exam practice: Part 3 (pp. 24–25)

A (p. 22)

Author of text:

Thubron, Colin (born 1939)

Left publishing to travel. Has written four highly praised novels and several award-winning travel books.

1 C; **2** G; **3** B; **4** D; **5** A; **6** F; **7** H

Vocabulary development (pp. 26–29)

A Words from the text (p. 26)

1 c; **2** i; **3** h; **4** g; **5** f; **6** d; **7** e; **8** j; **9** b; **10** a

B Descriptive verbs (p. 26)

1 spewed; **2** choked; **3** banked; **4** trickled; **5** jostled; **6** scattered; **7** bowled; **8** lingered

C Travelling and transport (p. 26)

People: conductor, motorist, skipper

Cars: bonnet, boot, convertible, hatchback, lay-by

Trains: buffet car, compartment, sidings, sleeping car

Boats: berth, deck, galley, gangplank, jetty, liner, mast, moorings, rudder, schooner

Planes: cockpit, fuselage, galley, landing-bay, runway, standby

D Prepositions (p. 27)

1 off; **2** against; **3** at; **4** behind; **5** below; **6** on; **7** out of; **8** over; **9** under; **10** up to

E Idioms and expressions with *go* (p. 28)

1 gone downhill

2 go halves

3 will go spare

4 went by the board

5 went to pieces

6 go the whole hog

7 goes off at a tangent

8 it went against the grain

9 went blank

10 went to great lengths

F **Phrasal verbs with** *go* (p. 28)

1 go about; **2** go on at; **3** go over; **4** went down with; **5** have (really) gone off; **6** went in for; **7** go along with; **8** go through with; **9** went through; **10** went for

G **Collocations with adjectives** (p. 29)

1 wild; **2** lost; **3** tall; **4** rude; **5** close; **6** far; **7** final; **8** foregone; **9** going; **10** narrow; **11** near; **12** long

H **Expressions with** *and* (p. 29)

1 bits and pieces	**7** peace and quiet
2 bright and early	**8** rack and ruin
3 give and take	**9** safe and sound
4 hustle and bustle	**10** short and sweet
5 odds and ends	**11** touch and go
6 part and parcel	**12** whys and wherefores

UNIT 4 **Larger than life**

Exam strategy: Part 4 (pp. 30–31)

A (p. 30)

Author of text:

Bennett, Alan (born 1934)

English dramatist, actor and director. He has written many plays for TV. 'The Lady in the Van', a true account of his experiences with a homeless woman who came to live in his street, is included in his autobiography.

B (p. 30)

caution = the quality of using great care and attention

neb = the peak of a cap

on the skew = not straight; sloping or twisted

peak = the flat curved part of a cap which sticks out in front above the eyes

went in for = made a habit of (doing); liked

expedient = something useful or helpful for a purpose

hem = the edge of a piece of cloth that is turned under and sewn down, especially the lower edge of a dress or skirt

fell foul of = got into trouble with

indignant = feeling surprised anger

D (p. 31)

Subject of text:

Dahl, Roald (1916–1990)

British children's author and short story writer. Born in Wales, of Norwegian parents. Among the most popular children's authors of all time. His stories are often anarchic and quite violent. Many of his books have been made into films. 'Boy' is autobiographical.

E (p. 31)

1 d; **2** c; **3** d; **4** c

F (p. 31)

1 a; **2** d

Exam practice: Part 4 (pp. 32–33)

A radical multimillionaire

Subject of text:

Roddick, Anita (born 1956)

Highly successful English retail entrepreneur. Founded 'The Body Shop' with her husband Thomas Gordon. The shops sell cosmetics made from natural materials. There are over 100 stores in the UK and at least twice as many in other countries.

1 B; **2** C; **3** A; **4** B; **5** B; **6** D; **7** D

Vocabulary development (pp. 34–37)

A **Similar but different** (p. 34)

1 shrugged; **2** crumpled; **3** skin; **4** breed; **5** barrage; **6** stick; **7** had; **8** scent; **9** giggle; **10** messy

B **Opposites** (p. 34)

1 a; **2** d; **3** e; **4** g; **5** h; **6** i; **7** c; **8** b; **9** f; **10** j

C **Character adjectives** (p. 35)

1 positive; **2** positive; **3** negative; **4** positive; **5** negative; **6** positive; **7** positive; **8** negative; **9** negative; **10** negative; **11** negative; **12** negative; **13** negative; **14** positive; **15** positive; **16** positive; **17** negative; **18** negative; **19** positive or negative; **20** positive; **21** negative; **22** positive; **23** negative; **24** positive

D **Idioms with parts of the body** (p. 35)
1 has got a good head on his shoulders
2 put his foot in it
3 didn't lift a finger
4 see eye to eye
5 're head over heels in love
6 keep your chin up
7 haven't (got) the guts
8 cost an arm and a leg
9 're (just) pulling your leg
10 is on its last legs

E **Expressions and idioms** (p. 36)

1 question	5 grain
2 call	6 rut
3 scratch	7 cuff
4 pinch	8 dumps

F **Phrasal verbs with _come_** (p. 36)
1 come out with
2 came across
3 come up against
4 come about
5 came through
6 came down
7 come round to
8 came into
9 come up with
10 comes/came across as
11 came down with
12 come up to

G **Similar words** (p. 37)
1 childlike = like a child. The other adjectives describe behaviour in adults which in some negative way resembles a child's.
2 canny = clever, careful and not easily deceived. The other adjectives are associated with kindness or goodness.
3 modest = having or expressing a lower opinion of one's own ability than is probably deserved. The other adjectives are all connected with arrogance.
4 planned = organised; pre-arranged. The other adjectives and expressions are associated with doing something on the spur of the moment, without planning for it in any way.
5 sane = healthy in mind; not mad. The other adjectives are all connected with madness.
6 skip = to move in a light, dancing way, with quick steps and jumps. The other verbs describe ways of moving with difficulty.
7 pressed = ironed; made flat. The other adjectives describe the state of material or clothes which are full of folds because they have been crushed.
8 jodhpurs = special trousers for horse riding. The other nouns refer to footwear.

9 tight = (for clothes), fitting part of the body very or too closely. The other adjectives describe clothes which are not tight and do not fit closely.
10 dawdle = to waste time; to move or do something very slowly. The other verbs describe ways of moving very fast or in a hurry.
11 vivacious = full of life and high spirits. The other adjectives are associated with tiredness.
12 down in the dumps = sad; depressed. The other expressions are associated with being very happy or pleased.
13 grin = to make a wide smile. The other verbs are connected with bad temper and unpleasant feelings.
14 squat = to sit on a surface with the knees bent and the legs drawn fully up under the body. The other verbs are ways of looking, not sitting.

H **Expressions with _come_** (p. 37)
1 come down to earth
2 take each day as it comes
3 do not know if I am coming or going
4 came/comes as no surprise
5 has been coming apart at the seams
6 came to life
7 came to a head
8 come clean
9 have (always) come easily
10 come what may

UNIT

5 | Sights and sounds

Exam strategy: Part 1 (pp. 38–39)

A (p. 38)
a
1 on; 2 to; 3 to; 4 at; 5 to; 6 with; 7 on; 8 of;
9 with; 10 on

b
1 f; 2 i; 3 j; 4 c; 5 h; 6 e; 7 g; 8 a; 9 b; 10 d

B (p. 39)
1 b; 2 b; 3 a; 4 b; 5 a; 6 b; 7 b; 8 a; 9 a; 10 b

Exam practice: Part 1 (pp. 40–41)

Becoming a pop idol (p. 40)
1 B; 2 D; 3 A; 4 C; 5 A; 6 D

Children's authors (p. 41)
7 D; 8 B; 9 A; 10 C; 11 C; 12 D

Digging for dinosaur fossils (p. 41)
13 D;   **14** C;   **15** A;   **16** B;   **17** D;   **18** C

Vocabulary development (pp. 42–45)

A Expressions and idioms connected with music (p. 42)

1 music;   **2** song;   **3** tune;   **4** drum;   **5** tune;   **6** song;
7 harping;   **8** fiddle;   **9** drum;   **10** tune

B Expressions with be (p. 42)

1 e;   **2** f;   **3** h;   **4** i;   **5** c;   **6** a;   **7** d;   **8** j;   **9** b;   **10** g

1 is/will be in for
2 are (always) at each others' throats
3 is/was at pains to
4 was in on
5 will be/is plain sailing
6 am up to my eyes
7 are after
8 were beside themselves
9 is/will be up against
10 will be/are over the hill

C Similar but different (p. 43)

1 thereby;   **2** meticulous;   **3** offence;   **4** ended up;
5 notwithstanding;   **6** stroke;   **7** sketch;   **8** stamp;
9 something;   **10** confronted

D Cinema and theatre terms (p. 43)

1 dubbed;   **2** prompt;   **3** clips;   **4** screenplay;
5 rehearsal, understudy;   **6** sketch, asides;   **7** trailer;
8 shoot, props;   **9** set, extras;   **10** fake

E Expressions and idioms with make and do (p. 44)

1 make;   **2** make;   **3** done;   **4** made;   **5** doing;
6 make;   **7** make;   **8** done;   **9** done;   **10** made

F Prepositions (p. 44)

1 on;   **2** off;   **3** in;   **4** under;   **5** By;   **6** below;   **7** at;
8 over;   **9** up;   **10** above

G Collocations (p. 45)

1 froze their blood
2 pulling your leg
3 strike lucky
4 melted (John's) heart
5 made a fortune
6 take sides
7 call (George's) bluff
8 catches my eye

H Phrasal verbs with run (p. 45)

1 ran into;   **2** running down;   **3** run over;
4 ran into;   **5** ran off;   **6** ran off with;
7 run out of;   **8** ran across/into

UNIT 6 The joys of learning

Exam strategy: Part 2 (pp. 46–47)

B (p. 46)

1 no;   **2** no;   **3** no
The answer to all three questions is no. The writer is being ironic when talking about the conditions under which the pupils are expected to play rugby. In fact, they do not enjoy playing rugby on a cold winter day while wearing inadequate clothing to protect them from the rain and winter weather.

D (p. 46)

1 The second text
2 The first text

E (p. 46)

The first text might come from a magazine, a book of essays or humorous articles, a novel, a biography or an autobiography.
The second text might come from a novel, a biography or autobiography.

F (p. 47)

1 probably true;   **2** probably true;   **3** probably true;
4 probably true

G (p. 47)

Students should underline the following:
1 *I have the greatest respect for the university and its 800 years of tireless intellectual toil*
2 *it seems to me that when a nation's industrial prowess has plunged so low that it is reliant on Korean firms for its future economic security, …*
3 *a tad indulgent in a country with three million unemployed and whose last great invention was cat's eyes?*
4 *but I must confess that I'm not entirely clear what it's for, now that Britain no longer needs colonial administrators who can quip in Latin.*

H (p. 47)

1 A;   **2** C

Exam practice: Part 2 (pp. 48–51)

Latin – hard labour? (p. 48)
1 B;   **2** D

Early memories (p. 49)
Author of text:
Lee, Laurie (1914–1997)
English poet and author. Educated in a village school in Stroud, Gloucestershire. His travels in many parts of the world are the subject of much of his writing. He is widely acclaimed for his evocation of his rural childhood in his autobiographical novel 'Cider with Rosie'.

3 A; **4** B

Chewing gum (p. 50)
5 C; **6** B

The new tutor (p. 51)
7 D; **8** B

Vocabulary development (pp. 52–55)

A Similar words (p. 52)
1 a expelled; b suspended
2 a diploma; b degree
3 a cramming; b revise
4 a trial; b competition
5 a subjects; b themes

B Similar but different (p. 52)
1 emit; **2** discharged; **3** imbue; **4** instil; **5** rebuffed;
6 extolled; **7** evade; **8** adopt

C Adjective and noun collocations (p. 53)
1 hard; **2** thorough; **3** broken; **4** incorrigible;
5 lasting; **6** formative

D Expressions to describe people (p. 53)
1 nosey; **2** stuffed; **3** smart; **4** live; **5** armchair;
6 soft; **7** fair-weather; **8** wet

E Expressions with *run* (p. 53)
1 ran him to ground/earth
2 run away with the idea/notion
3 runs counter to
4 My blood ran cold
5 were running riot

F Words connected with light and water (p. 54)
Light: gleam, glint, glow, sparkle, twinkle, wink
Water: drip, gush, pour, spill, sprinkle, trickle

G Similar but different (p. 54)
1 thorough; **2** assuming; **3** put; **4** overdue;
5 helping out; **6** refrain; **7** shouted;
8 dependent on; **9** incentive; **10** provision

H Prepositions (p. 55)
1 on; **2** to; **3** through; **4** on; **5** at; **6** on; **7** in;
8 on; **9** in; **10** by

I Phrasal verbs with *fall* (p. 55)
1 falling over; **2** fell for; **3** fell out; **4** fell behind;
5 fell through; **6** fall in with; **7** fell on;
8 didn't fall for; **9** fell about; **10** fell apart

UNIT
7 | **All in a day's work**

Exam strategy: Part 3 (pp. 56–57)

B (p. 56)
which = *several key technologies*
this marvel of science = *virtual reality*
this = *somewhere completely different*
one = *a place*
ones = *goggles*
them = *complex tasks*
these = *virtual reality cockpits*
them = *pilots*
the latter = *the patients*
this sphere = *the field of virtual reality technology*

D (p. 57)
1 B; **2** D; **3** C; **4** A

Exam practice: Part 3 (pp. 58–59)

1 F; **2** H; **3** C; **4** G; **5** D; **6** A; **7** E

Vocabulary development (pp. 60–63)

A Jobs and equipment (p. 60)
a
1 easel; **2** chisel; **3** tripod; **4** spanner; **5** scalpel

b
1 E; **2** A; **3** B; **4** D; **5** C

B Aspects of employment (p. 60)
1 redundancy package; **2** petty cash; **3** freelance;
4 workload; **5** the dole; **6** merger; **7** pension;
8 workforce; **9** overtime, backlog; **10** trade union

C Common work-related expressions (p. 61)
1 will show you the ropes
2 are in the black
3 have entered into negotiations
4 gets a foot on the ladder
5 is not within my field
6 take up a new post
7 is a dogsbody
8 was passed over for promotion
9 a breach of contract
10 pulled rank

D Phrasal verbs with *break* (p. 61)
1 broke off; 2 break up; 3 break up; 4 broke out;
5 broke into; 6 break in on; 7 broke out;
8 broken down; 9 broke through; 10 broke away;
11 breaking down; 12 broke out

E Similar but different (p. 62)
1 cluttered; 2 not; 3 speculation; 4 beneficial;
5 grievance; 6 scope; 7 Were; 8 trends

F Collocations with adjectives (p. 62)
1 vicious; 2 sure-fire; 3 skeleton; 4 rough; 5 snap;
6 flying; 7 golden; 8 star; 9 dead-end; 10 vested

G Similar but different (p. 63)
1 bones; 2 waffle; 3 virtual; 4 harm; 5 out;
6 smuggle; 7 fell; 8 off; 9 out; 10 leave

H Prepositions (p. 63)
1 in; 2 on; 3 out; 4 on; 5 in; 6 about; 7 on;
8 off; 9 through; 10 for

UNIT

8 Crimes and misdemeanours

Exam strategy: Part 4 (pp. 64–65)

A (p. 64)
Author of text:
James, P.D. (born 1920)
Popular English thriller writer, born in Oxford. One of the new 'Queens of Crime'.

B (p. 64)
1 Yes, she is suggestible. The girl believes that she can sense the 'Whistler' following her. *The creature, man or beast, crouching in the undergrowth was already sniffing her fear, waiting until her panic broke. Then she would hear the crash of the breaking bushes, his pounding feet, feel his panting breath hot on her neck.*

2 No, she is not walking through a built-up area in a city. The text mentions: 'the soft, rich-smelling earth', 'the undergrowth', 'the breaking bushes'.

3 No, it is the girl's imagination that leads her to believe that there is someone hiding in the bushes. This impression is given to the reader by the use of the words 'would hear'. *She would hear the crash of the breaking bushes …*

4 No, her parents do not know what she has been doing tonight. *Please God, let me get safely home and I'll never lie again.*

5 Yes, she is out later than usual. *I'll always leave on time.* This suggests that she did not, in fact, leave on time.

6 Yes, the figure ahead of her may not be as innocent and comforting as she thinks. The writer implies that the appearance of the figure is too good to be true; that the figure appeared from nowhere and it is unlikely that someone else would be out walking so late. *And then, miraculously, her prayer was answered. Suddenly, about thirty yards ahead of her, there was a woman. She didn't question how, so mysteriously, this slim, slow-walking figure had materialised.*

C (p. 65)
He was afraid of the dark walk up the drive to the house.

D (p. 65)
1 no; 2 no; 3 He would not have understood the boy's real fear. 4 his parents

E (p. 65)
C

F (p. 65)
1 D; 2 B

Exam practice: Part 4 (pp. 66–67)

The origins of the detective stories.
Subjects of text:
Poe, Edgar Allan (1809–1849)
American poet and story writer. He wrote highly original, weird, fantastic stories often dwelling on the macabre. Stories like 'Murders in the Rue Morgue', with original, intricate plots, are considered to have laid the pattern for the detective story.

Christie, Dame Agatha (1891–1979)
Immensely popular British writer of detective fiction.
Wrote brilliantly constructed plots with ingenious
psychological twists.

Doyle, Sir Arthur Conan (1859–1930)
British author, best known as the creator of the
detective, Sherlock Holmes. Born in Scotland and
studied medicine at Edinburgh University. Said to
have modelled deductive powers of Holmes on the
Edinburgh surgeon Sir Joseph Bell, under whom
Conan Doyle studied.

1 C; **2** D; **3** C; **4** B; **5** B; **6** D; **7** D

Vocabulary development (pp. 68–71)

A Types of crime (p. 68)
1 libel; **2** forgery; **3** shoplifting; **4** arson;
5 manslaughter; **6** conspiracy; **7** trespass; **8** bribery

B Legal terms (p. 68)
1 was sentenced to
2 reached/returned a verdict
3 fined (£200) for
4 arrest (the man) for
5 was/had been involved in
6 banned (the man) from
7 sue (her employers) for
8 charged with

C Adjective and noun collocations (p. 69)
1 besetting; **2** near; **3** marked; **4** foul; **5** spot;
6 ill-gotten; **7** rough; **8** put-up; **9** sharp; **10** funny

D Similar but different (p. 69)
1 eliminated; **2** recourse; **3** disposed; **4** slope;
5 fugitive; **6** slightest; **7** reprieved; **8** wave;
9 sentenced; **10** mounting; **11** loitering; **12** alleged

E Prepositions (p. 70)
1 under; **2** by; **3** up; **4** behind; **5** above; **6** for;
7 at; **8** on; **9** from; **10** in; **11** off; **12** out of

F Phrasal verbs with *get* (p. 70)
1 got round; **2** get (her) off; **3** getting up to;
4 got out of; **5** get along; **6** get at; **7** got down to;
8 get away with

G Similar but different (p. 71)
1 foul; **2** close; **3** shot; **4** pack; **5** blessing; **6** low;
7 rough; **8** sound; **9** large; **10** run

H Expressions connected with crime (p. 71)
1 b; **2** a; **3** a; **4** b; **5** a; **6** b; **7** b; **8** b; **9** a; **10** a

Exam practice 1

Part 1 (pp. 72–73)

A troubled teenager (p. 72)
1 B; **2** D; **3** A; **4** D; **5** D; **6** A

Mrs Bixby (p. 73)
7 C; **8** C; **9** B; **10** D; **11** C; **12** D

Stranded in a cave (p. 73)
13 B; **14** D; **15** B; **16** B; **17** A; **18** C

Part 2 (pp. 74–77)

What exactly is music? (p. 74)
19 D; **20** D;

A prizewinning novel (p. 75)
21 B; **22** D

A walk through the Scottish National Gallery (p. 76)
23 C; **24** D

The antique dealer (p. 77)
25 D; **26** B

Part 3 (pp. 78–79)
27 H; **28** G; **29** E; **30** A; **31** F; **32** D; **33** C

Part 4 (pp. 80–81)
34 A; **35** B; **36** C; **37** C; **38** D; **39** B; **40** D

UNIT
9 **The science of life**

Exam strategy: Part 1 (pp. 82–83)

A (p. 82)
1 A; **2** C; **3** C; **4** A; **5** D; **6** C; **7** C; **8** B

B (pp. 82–83)
1 D; **2** D; **3** A; **4** C; **5** A; **6** C; **7** D; **8** D

C Intelligent life in space? (p. 83)
1 B; **2** A; **3** C; **4** B; **5** D

Exam practice: Part 1 (pp. 84–85)

Optimism and pessimism (p. 84)
1 D; **2** B; **3** A; **4** C; **5** D; **6** A

House-hunting (p. 84)
7 B; **8** C; **9** D; **10** C; **11** A; **12** B

Leadership qualities (p. 85)
13 B; **14** A; **15** C; **16** D; **17** B; **18** B

Vocabulary development (pp. 86–89)

A Processes (p. 86)
1 g; **2** h; **3** e; **4** d; **5** c; **6** a; **7** b; **8** f

B Adjective and noun collocations (p. 86)
1 closed book; **2** necessary evil; **3** bitter pill;
4 knotty problem; **5** impassioned plea;
6 prime suspect; **7** blind alley; **8** graphic detail;
9 acid test; **10** burning question

C Similar but different (p. 87)
1 proximity; **2** infancy; **3** threw; **4** cut; **5** oversee;
6 impervious; **7** principle; **8** set about; **9** tinkering;
10 allied

D Verb and noun collocations (p. 87)
1 e; **2** i; **3** a; **4** g; **5** b; **6** j; **7** f; **8** d; **9** c; **10** h

E Phrasal verbs with *put* (p. 88)
1 put down to; **2** put across; **3** put in for;
4 put aside; **5** put up with; **6** put back; **7** put (it) to;
8 putting (him) down; **9** put forward;
10 put (him) down as

F Idioms and expressions with *put* (p. 88)
1 put paid to
2 put the record straight
3 are putting out feelers
4 put the new recruit through his paces
5 put in an appearance
6 put down roots
7 put all the other students in the shade
8 was put off the scent
9 put me through the mill
10 put me in the picture

G Prepositions (p. 89)
1 on; **2** for; **3** from, to; **4** on; **5** in; **6** for;
7 about; **8** in

H Expressions and idioms (p. 89)
1 sweep; **2** point; **3** poke; **4** hand; **5** world;
6 blue; **7** dumps; **8** moon

UNIT 10 True to life

Exam strategy: Part 2 (pp. 90–91)

A (p. 90)
2

B (p. 91)
1 A; **2** D

D (p. 91)
1 Question 2; **2** Question 1

Exam practice: Part 2 (pp. 92–95)

My mother (p. 92)
1 A; **2** B

Is Prince William related to Shakespeare? (p. 93)
Subject of text:
Shakespeare, William (1564–1616)
English playwright, poet, actor. Born in Stratford upon
Avon. Went to London as a young man and spent the
next 25 years there as an actor and playwright. He
wrote poetry, including 154 sonnets, which are
considered among the world's finest. Many attempts
have been made to identify the mysterious people who
appear in them, such as 'The Dark Lady'.

3 D; **4** C

Rembrandt (p. 94)
5 A; **6** C

A portrait (p. 95)
7 C; **8** A

Vocabulary development (pp. 96–99)

A Idioms with comparisons (p. 96)
1 a post; **2** a bat; **3** a coot; **4** a hatter; **5** a mouse;
6 life; **7** sin; **8** toast; **9** a sheet; **10** rain; **11** houses;
12 the hills; **13** Punch; **14** a cucumber; **15** a whistle;
16 chalk and cheese; **17** a fiddle; **18** a daisy;
19 crystal; **20** a new pin

B Expressions with parts of the body (p. 96)
1 head; **2** hand; **3** neck; **4** heel; **5** back; **6** bone;
7 hair; **8** foot; **9** finger; **10** face

C **Similar but different** (p. 97)
1 tried; **2** cling; **3** hand; **4** indifferent; **5** found;
6 foreign; **7** competent; **8** frame; **9** Considering;
10 hinted

D **Adjective and noun collocations** (p. 97)
1 wishful thinking; **2** a mixed blessing; **3** a raw deal;
4 second nature; **5** an olive branch; **6** a far cry;
7 rose-coloured spectacles; **8** a sweeping statement

E **Phrasal verbs with** *look* (p. 98)
1 look to; **2** look out; **3** look into; **4** looked down
on; **5** looked over; **6** look in on; **7** looked on;
8 look up to

F **Expressions with** *look* (p. 98)
1 look before you leap
2 looked him up and down
3 looked daggers at her
4 looks down her nose at her husband's family
5 look a gift horse in the mouth
6 look on the bright side
7 look the worse for wear
8 look to his laurels

G **Prepositions** (p. 99)
1 about; **2** at; **3** with; **4** about; **5** of; **6** on; **7** at;
8 to; **9** with; **10** on

H **Expressions and idioms with the weather** (p. 99)
1 cast; **2** head; **3** rainy; **4** storm; **5** took;
6 wind; **7** heavy; **8** under; **9** wind; **10** weather

UNIT
11 **Health matters**

Exam strategy: Part 3 (pp. 100–101)

A (p. 100)
1 E; **2** B; **3** A; **4** C

B (p. 101)
Paragraph D is not needed.

Exam practice: Part 3 (pp. 102–103)

1 F; **2** D; **3** B; **4** H; **5** C ; **6** A; **7** G

Vocabulary development (pp. 104–107)

A **Parts of the body (1)** (p. 104)
1 skull; **2** collarbone; **3** ribs; **4** lungs;
5 heart; **6** kidneys

B **Parts of the body (2)** (p. 104)
1 vital organs; **2** gland; **3** joints; **4** liver;
5 bladder; **6** womb; **7** veins; **8** tendon;
9 spine; **10** intestine

C **Expressions with parts of the body** (p. 105)
1 b; **2** b; **3** a; **4** b; **5** a; **6** b; **7** a; **8** b; **9** b; **10** a

D **Expressions with** *finger* (p. 105)
1 e; **2** a; **3** c; **4** f; **5** d; **6** b

E **Phrasal verbs with** *make* (p. 106)
1 make up; **2** makes up for; **3** made out;
4 made for; **5** made off with; **6** made off;
7 make out; **8** he was making (it) up

F **Similar but different** (p. 106)
1 up; **2** on; **3** loath; **4** on; **5** to; **6** on; **7** under;
8 to; **9** with; **10** on; **11** in; **12** on

G **Verbs** (p. 107)
1 summon; **2** gobbled; **3** put; **4** whip; **5** take;
6 gave; **7** foisted; **8** equate; **9** cling; **10** thwarted

H **Similar words** (p. 107)
1 a; **2** b; **3** a; **4** b; **5** b; **6** a; **7** b; **8** b

UNIT
12 **The fruits of technology**

Exam strategy: Part 4 (pp. 108–109)

A (p. 108)
1 a arguably; b indisputably
2 a implied; b stated
3 a can provoke; b invariably provokes
4 a It may be that; b It is a fact that

B (pp. 108–109)
1 D; **2** B; **3** C; **4** C

Exam practice: Part 4 (pp. 110–111)

Mobile phones
1 A;　**2** A;　**3** D;　**4** C;　**5** C;　**6** B;　**7** A

Vocabulary development (pp. 112–115)

A Descriptive adjectives (p. 112)
a
1 blunt;　**2** tarnished;　**3** tattered;　**4** chipped;
5 tangled;　**6** shattered;　**7** faded;　**8** warped;
9 dented;　**10** ripped

b
1 was dented/shattered;　**2** tarnished;　**3** chip;
4 were shattered;　**5** ripped;　**6** blunt;　**7** warped;
8 fading

B Phrasal verbs with *give* (p. 113)
1 gave out;　**2** give off;　**3** had given away;
4 given (so much) of;　**5** given over to;　**6** give up;
7 give in;　**8** given up on

C Components, tools and equipment (p. 113)
1 headboard　Topic: electrics
2 hardboard　Topic: computers
3 protractor　Topic: gardening
4 sieve　Topic: cycling
5 shutter　Topic: telephoning
6 spanner　Topic: driving
7 screwdriver　Topic: cooking
8 hinge　Topic: photography

D Similar but different (p. 113)
1 accordance;　**2** folding;　**3** tapered off;　**4** brand;
5 call;　**6** power;　**7** peak;　**8** sets

E Expressions with *give* (p. 114)
1 is given to
2 gave the game away
3 to give him his due
4 gives me the creeps
5 give them a run for their money
6 give the lie to (rumours that the company is on the rocks)
7 gives them the edge over
8 gave vent to
9 have given rise to
10 gave me the slip

F Similar words (p. 115)
1 b;　**2** a;　**3** a;　**4** a;　**5** a;　**6** b;　**7** b;　**8** a

G More expressions with *make* and *do* (p. 115)
1 make;　**2** do;　**3** make;　**4** make;　**5** made;　**6** do;
7 make;　**8** make;　**9** do;　**10** made

UNIT 13 Mind over matter

Exam strategy: Part 1 (pp. 116–117)

A (p. 116)
1 b;　**2** b;　**3** a;　**4** a;　**5** b;　**6** b;　**7** b;　**8** b

B (p. 116)
1 near;　**2** good;　**3** not;　**4** full;　**5** foreseeable;
6 Roughly;　**7** standards;　**8** low

C The robots are coming (p. 117)
1 C;　**2** D;　**3** A;　**4** C;　**5** B;　**6** D

Exam practice: Part 1 (pp. 118–119)

A magazine editor (p. 118)
1 B;　**2** C;　**3** A;　**4** D;　**5** C;　**6** B

The snakeman (p. 119)
7 C;　**8** B;　**9** A;　**10** D;　**11** C;　**12** A

The survivors (p. 119)
13 C;　**14** B;　**15** D;　**16** A;　**17** B;　**18** D

Vocabulary development (pp. 120–123)

A Expressions with *time* (p. 120)
1 from time to time
2 there's no time like the present
3 at the best of times
4 for the time being
5 keep up with the times
6 pressed for time
7 in your own good time
8 am killing time
9 in the nick of time
10 time will tell
11 play for time
12 in no time
13 behind the times
14 is doing/did/has done time
15 time after time

B Phrases with *turn* (p. 120)
1 i;　**2** c;　**3** j;　**4** b;　**5** a;　**6** f;　**7** e;　**8** g;　**9** h;　**10** d

C **Phrasal verbs with *turn*** (p. 121)
1 turned on; **2** turned out of; **3** turned (me) off;
4 turned (the boy) over; **5** turned against;
6 turned (him) down; **7** turned up; **8** turn to;
9 turned into; **10** turned away from

D **Verb and noun collocations** (p. 121)
1 picking holes in the scheme; **2** kicked up a fuss;
3 raised the roof; **4** stick to your guns; **5** take sides;
6 pass the buck; **7** missed the boat; **8** sit on the
fence; **9** hit the headlines; **10** pull her punches

E **Expressions and idioms** (p. 122)
1 run riot; **2** taken a toll on; **3** bury the hatchet;
4 clear the air; **5** blow her top; **6** carry the can;
7 get a grip; **8** has drawn a blank; **9** feel the pinch;
10 weather the storm

F **Fixed phrases and idioms** (p. 123)
1 figment; **2** verge; **3** clue; **4** parcel; **5** sour;
6 wildest; **7** scared; **8** gist; **9** between; **10** chew

G **Prepositions** (p. 123)
1 above; **2** out; **3** on; **4** up; **5** on; **6** out;
7 around; **8** in; **9** on; **10** in

UNIT

14 **The information age**

Exam strategy: Part 2 (pp. 124–125)

B (p. 124)
It was written for people who want to lost weight. The
purpose of the text is to persuade.

C (p. 124)
1 b; **2** c; **3** a

D (p. 125)
1 C; **2** A

Exam practice: Part 2 (pp. 126–129)

Electrical appliances (p. 126)
1 B; **2** B

An ergonomic screen (p. 127)
3 D; **4** D

Please continue to hold (p. 128)
5 C; **6** B

Mobile phones – curse or blessing? (p. 129)
7 C; **8** C

Vocabulary development (pp. 130–133)

A **Verb and noun collocations** (p. 130)
1 h; **2** e; **3** b; **4** a; **5** g; **6** d; **7** f; **8** c

B **Expressions** (p. 130)
1 changed his tune
2 met her match
3 serves you right
4 take your pick
5 pulling their weight
6 have taken leave of her senses
7 earned his keep
8 driving me mad
9 call his bluff
10 follow in his footsteps

C **Phrasal verbs** (p. 131)
1 get through to; **2** mulled over; **3** jack in;
4 rake up; **5** happen on/upon; **6** bring out;
7 conned me into buying the car; **8** picked up on;
9 iron out; **10** happened on/upon; **11** beef up;
12 have blown up; **13** is on to; **14** were borne out

D **Describing ways of speaking and looking**
(pp. 131–132)
a
Ways of speaking: bark, drone, gasp, sob, twitter
Ways of looking: beam, gape, grimace, pout, scowl

b
1 sobbed; **2** gape; **3** beamed; **4** twittering;
5 barked; **6** gasped; **7** grimaced; **8** droned;
9 scowled; **10** pouted

E **Verbs of movement** (p. 132)
1 bounce; **2** sag; **3** glided; **4** floated; **5** rotated;
6 pivots; **7** tilt; **8** adjust

F **Computer parts** (p. 132)
1 monitor; **2** speaker; **3** keyboard; **4** mouse;
5 disk drive

G **Prepositions** (p. 133)
1 on; **2** up; **3** into; **4** off; **5** to; **6** at; **7** on;
8 up; **9** on; **10** with

H Similar words (p. 133)
1 a; **2** a; **3** a; **4** b; **5** b; **6** b; **7** b; **8** a

UNIT 15 It's all in the genes

Exam strategy: Part 3 (pp. 134–135)

A (p. 134)
1 C; **2** E; **3** A; **4** B

Exam practice: Part 3 (pp. 136–137)

1 D; **2** H; **3** C; **4** E; **5** G; **6** F; **7** A

Vocabulary development (pp. 138–141)

A Prepositions (p. 138)
1 on/in; **2** from; **3** off; **4** for; **5** for; **6** on; **7** to;
8 with; **9** for; **10** with; **11** on; **12** off; **13** on;
14 on

B Similar but different (p. 138)
1 other; **2** lends; **3** plead; **4** rate; **5** influence;
6 threw; **7** incited; **8** suppress

C Phrasal verbs with *lay* and *set* (p. 139)
1 set her off; **2** laid down; **3** laid into me; **4** lay off;
5 lay this problem on you; **6** setting about;
7 laid off; **8** set back; **9** set to; **10** set aside

D Common idioms and expressions (p. 139)
1 disguise; **2** blot; **3** drop; **4** gift; **5** tower; **6** pack;
7 stone; **8** tip

E Similar words (p. 140)
1 a except; **b** but for
2 a In the light of; **b** On account of
3 a assuming; **b** considering
4 a in view of; **b** in case
5 a at the behest of; **b** on the part of
6 a thereby; **b** whereby

F Expressions (p. 140)
1 rub it in
2 call it quits
3 has (got) several irons in the fire
4 what makes her tick
5 play it by ear
6 like it or lump it
7 it makes no odds
8 hit it off
9 It beats me
10 it's back to the drawing board

G Adjectives (p. 141)
a
1 g; **2** h; **3** i; **4** f; **5** b; **6** j; **7** e; **8** a; **9** d; **10** c

b
1 tortuous; **2** tempting; **3** breezy; **4** promiscuous;
5 pointless; **6** flawed; **7** risible; **8** irresistible;
9 listless; **10** sloppy

H Verb phrases (p. 141)
1 spells; **2** tampered; **3** bear; **4** make; **5** take;
6 catch

UNIT 16 The shadow of the past

Exam strategy: Part 4 (pp. 142–143)

A (p. 142)
2

C (p. 142)
B

D (p. 143)
1 C; **2** D

Exam practice: Part 4 (pp. 144–145)

1 B; **2** C; **3** C; **4** D; **5** D; **6** D; **7** A

Vocabulary development (pp. 146–149)

A **Common expressions** (p. 146)

a
1 g; **2** i; **3** h; **4** f; **5** e; **6** d; **7** b; **8** c; **9** a; **10** j

b
1 settled their differences
2 has a crush on
3 set the world alight
4 come in handy
5 Buoyed up
6 pricked up my ears
7 bitten off more than he/she can chew
8 jumped at the chance
9 was not cut out for
10 to give him/her his/her due

B **Collocations** (p. 147)
1 f; **2** g; **3** j; **4** e; **5** b; **6** h; **7** d; **8** a; **9** i; **10** c

C **Similar but different** (p. 147)
1 driven; **2** pace; **3** within; **4** scale; **5** buoyed;
6 outcome; **7** prevalent; **8** sophisticated;
9 borrow; **10** hold

D **Expressions** (p. 148)
1 swim with the tide
2 brought it home to me
3 have broken new ground
4 burning the midnight oil
5 cut no ice with
6 to do the spadework
7 go by the board
8 have no truck with

E **Colours** (p. 148)
1 blue; **2** black; **3** red; **4** black; **5** red; **6** green;
7 blue; **8** green

F **Phrasal verbs with** *bring* (p. 149)
1 brought out; **2** brought (Sam and Ella) together;
3 bring up; **4** brought about; **5** brings back;
6 brought down; **7** has been brought back;
8 brought off

G **Prepositions** (p. 149)
1 on; **2** to; **3** in; **4** on; **5** in; **6** on; **7** in; **8** along;
9 through; **10** down

Exam practice 2

Part 1 (pp. 150–151)

Ordeal in the Highlands (p. 150)
1 C; **2** B; **3** D; **4** A; **5** B; **6** D

Stress at work (p. 150)
7 D; **8** B; **9** A; **10** B; **11** D; **12** C

Hector Berlioz (p. 151)
13 D; **14** C; **15** A; **16** B; **17** A; **18** D

Part 2 (pp. 152–155)

Unidentified Flying Objects (p. 152)
19 C; **20** C

On-line auctions (p. 153)
21 B; **22** C

Genetically modified crops (p. 154)
23 C; **24** B

Hibernation (p. 155)
25 C; **26** A

Part 3 (pp. 156–157)

27 F; **28** G; **29** E; **30** D; **31** H; **32** A; **33** B

Part 4 (pp. 158–159)

34 C; **35** A; **36** D; **37** C; **38** A; **39** D; **40** B

Progress Tests: Answer Key

Progress Test 1 (Units 1–4)

1 A; **2** C; **3** C; **4** B; **5** D; **6** A; **7** A; **8** A; **9** D;
10 C; **11** B; **12** C; **13** C; **14** C; **15** C; **16** A; **17** D;
18 B; **19** C; **20** B; **21** A; **22** C; **23** B; **24** C;
25 D; **26** D; **27** C; **28** D; **29** B; **30** A; **31** B;
32 D; **33** B; **34** A; **35** C; **36** B; **37** A; **38** B;
39 C; **40** A; **41** C; **42** D; **43** A; **44** A; **45** A

Progress Test 2 (Units 5–8)

1 C; **2** A; **3** C; **4** D; **5** D; **6** B; **7** B; **8** A; **9** B;
10 A; **11** B; **12** A; **13** B; **14** D; **15** A; **16** C; **17** B;
18 B; **19** D; **20** C; **21** A; **22** A; **23** C; **24** D;
25 A; **26** C; **27** D; **28** A; **29** D; **30** A; **31** A;
32 C; **33** C; **34** D; **35** B; **36** D; **37** B; **38** D;
39 A; **40** A; **41** C; **42** D; **43** D; **44** B; **45** A

Progress Test 3 (Units 9–12)

1 D; **2** B; **3** A; **4** C; **5** B; **6** B; **7** C; **8** A; **9** B;
10 D; **11** A; **12** C; **13** A; **14** D; **15** D; **16** C;
17 B; **18** A; **19** B; **20** C; **21** D; **22** D; **23** A;
24 B; **25** A; **26** C; **27** D; **28** D; **29** B; **30** C;
31 B; **32** C; **33** A; **34** A; **35** A; **36** C; **37** A;
38 D; **39** C; **40** B; **41** C; **42** A; **43** D; **44** C;
45 D

Progress Test 4 (Units 13–16)

1 A; **2** B; **3** A; **4** A; **5** A; **6** C; **7** D; **8** B; **9** B;
10 D; **11** C; **12** B; **13** A; **14** B; **15** B; **16** C; **17** C;
18 D; **19** A; **20** B; **21** C; **22** C; **23** D; **24** B;
25 C; **26** C; **27** C; **28** D; **29** B; **30** C; **31** B;
32 D; **33** D; **34** B; **35** C; **36** B; **37** C; **38** B;
39 A; **40** D; **41** B; **42** A; **43** D; **44** C; **45** D